Navigating Health Insurance

Your Comprehensive Guide to Wellness and Financial Security

Patricia Kenyon

Table of contents

Introduction

In a world where the expense of healthcare can be as unpredictable as the weather, and the complexity of insurance policies frequently resembles a maze, the need for a dependable compass to navigate you through the labyrinth of health insurance has never been more vital.

Welcome to "Navigating Health Insurance," your trusty companion on the path to understanding, managing, and utilizing the potential of health insurance.

Imagine a life where you're free from the concern of medical bills building up, where you confidently pick the healthcare services you need without fear of financial ruin, and where your family's well-being is preserved against the unforeseen twists and turns of life. This book is your access to that universe.

Health insurance is not simply a safety net; it's your key to unlocking a better, more secure future. However, it may be as daunting as it is vital. The terminology might feel like a foreign language, the options are daunting, and the paperwork is a maze of uncertainty. But fear not! In the pages that follow, we will demystify the world of health insurance.

Together, we'll explore the principles of health insurance, analyze the terminology, and share insider methods and insights that will enable you to make knowledgeable decisions. Whether you're a young professional just starting out, a family navigating the complexity of coverage, or a retiree seeking peace of mind, this book is your route to financial stability and peace of mind.

Get ready to embark on a journey, where you'll learn the knowledge and confidence to take care of your health, your money, and your future. "Navigating Health Insurance" is your passport to a future where health insurance isn't a burden but a tool for a better, healthier tomorrow. So, let's begin this amazing voyage together!

Chapter 1: What Is Health Insurance

Health insurance is an arrangement in which an insurance company promises to pay for part or all of your medical expenditures in exchange for a monthly premium payment.

If you're young, healthy, and lucky, the monthly premium may exceed the price of your insurance.

If you (or someone in your family) have a recurrent ailment that needs treatment or develops one, are hurt in an accident, or get an illness, you may probably incur medical expenditures that you cannot reasonably afford.

Health insurance is a contract between a firm and a consumer. The employer offers to pay all or a portion of the insured person's healthcare bills in return for payment of a monthly premium.

The contract is generally a one-year arrangement, during which the insurer will be liable for paying particular expenditures connected to illness, accident, pregnancy, or preventative treatment.

Health insurance agreements in the U.S. often come with restrictions to coverage including:

-A deductible that requires the customer to pay some healthcare expenditures "out-of-pocket" up to a maximum amount before the business coverage begins.

-One or more co-payments that require the customer to pay a specified part of the cost for certain services or procedures.

-Health insurance compensates most medical and surgical expenditures and preventative care costs incurred by the covered person in return for a monthly premium payment.

Generally, the larger the monthly premium is the smaller the out-of-pocket expenditures are to the insured.

-Virtually all health plans include deductibles and copays but these out-of-pocket expenditures are now restricted by federal law.

-Since 2010, the Affordable Care Act has barred insurance companies from rejecting coverage to individuals with previous diseases and has enabled children to remain on their parent's health plan until they reach the age of

-Medicare, Medicaid, and the Children's Health Insurance Program (CHIP) are government health insurance policies that provide coverage to elderly, handicapped, and low-income people.

Chapter 2: How Health Insurance Works

In the United States, health insurance is tough to negotiate. It is a company with a variety of regional and national rivals whose coverage, pricing, and availability vary from state to state and even by county.

About half of the population receives health insurance coverage as a job benefit, with premiums partially reimbursed by the employer.

The expense to the employer is tax-deductible to the payer, and the benefits to the employee are tax-free, with specific exclusions for S company workers.

Self-employed persons, freelancers, and gig workers can obtain insurance directly on their own. The Affordable Care Act of 2010, widely dubbed Obamacare, authorized the construction of a nationwide database, named HealthCare.gov, which allows consumers to search for basic plans from private insurers that are accessible where they reside. The prices of the coverage are subsidized for taxpayers whose incomes are between 100% and 400% of the federal poverty line.

Some, but not all, states built their own versions of HealthCare.gov that are targeted to their inhabitants.

People over the age of 65 and those with impairments, End-Stage Renal Disease, or ALS qualify to receive federally financed treatment through Medicare, while families whose earnings are near the poverty level are eligible for subsidized Medicaid coverage.

Chapter 3: Types of Health Insurance

Health insurance may be tough to negotiate in the U.S.

So-called managed care insurance plans compel consumers to seek their care from a network of certified healthcare providers. If patients seek care outside the network, they must pay a greater proportion of the cost.
The insurer may even deny payment outright for services received out of network.

Many managed care plans—for example, health maintenance organizations (HMOs) and point-of-service plans (POS)—require patients to pick a primary care physician who monitors the patient's care, makes recommendations regarding treatment, and offers referrals for medical specialists.

Preferred provider organizations (PPOs), by contrast, don't require referrals but do establish cheaper fees for using in-network practitioners and services.

Insurance companies may refuse coverage for certain treatments that were obtained without preauthorization. They may deny payment for name-brand pharmaceuticals if a generic version or equivalent prescription is available at a cheaper cost.

All these criteria should be included in the documentation given by the insurance provider. It's recommended to verify with the firm directly before spending a large expenditure.

Who Needs Health Insurance?
The basic answer is everyone. Health insurance compensates for the costs of minor medical difficulties and serious ones, including surgery and treatment for life-

threatening diseases and disabling disorders.

Chapter 4: What Are Copays, Deductibles, and Coinsurance?

Most health insurance plans demand their clients to pay up some of the expenses of their coverage in several ways:

The deductible is the amount that the customer must pay out of pocket every year before the insurer begins to fund the costs. This is currently capped by federal law.

Copays are predetermined costs that subscribers must pay for certain services like medical visits and prescription medicines even after the deductible is reached.

Coinsurance is the proportion of healthcare expenditures that the insured must pay even after they've met the deductible (but only until they reach the out-of-pocket limit for the year).

Insurance plans with higher out-of-pocket payments often have lower monthly rates. When looking for plans, evaluate the benefit of lower monthly payments against the possible danger of big out-of-pocket spending in the case of a serious sickness or accident.

High-Deductible Health Plans (HDHP)
One increasingly common kind of health insurance is the high-deductible health plan (HDHP). These plans feature bigger deductibles and lower monthly costs.

Their customers are the only ones qualified to create a Health Savings Account (HSA) that offers large federal tax benefits.

For 2023, the IRS defines a high-deductible health plan as one that has deductibles of at least $1,500 for an individual or $3,000 for a family. Total out-of-pocket maximums are $7,500 for a person and $15,000 for a family.

For 2024, a high-deductible health plan is one that includes deductibles of at least $1,600 for an individual or $3,100 for a family. Total out-of-pocket maximums are $8,050 for an individual and also $16,100 for a family.

High-deductible health plans provide a unique advantage in that if you have one, you're able to open—and contribute pretax income to—a health savings account, which may be used to pay for eligible medical expenditures. These programs give a threefold tax benefit in that:

Contributions are tax-deductible
Contributions increase on a tax-deferred basis
Qualified withdrawals for healthcare costs are tax-free

Federal Health Insurance Plans

Not all health insurance in the US is offered by private firms. Medicare, Medicaid, and the Children's Health Insurance Program (CHIP) are government health insurance programs that offer coverage to elderly, handicapped, and low-income people.

Chapter 5: What is Open Enrollment For Health Insurance in 2024

Open enrollment for 2024 health insurance plans begins November 1, 2023, and concludes on January 15, 2024.

This is when you may buy individual and family insurance plans through the Affordable Care Act (ACA) marketplace or your state's marketplace. To acquire coverage that starts as of January 1, 2024, you have to sign up by December 15, 2023.

If you get insurance via your employment, termed group health insurance, your company chooses when you can enroll or make changes to your coverage.

Some states have varied dates for health insurance open enrollment. There are longer open enrollment periods in California,

Kentucky, Massachusetts, New Jersey, Rhode Island and Washington, D.C. In contrast, Idaho starts and concludes its open enrollment period sooner than other states. Where you reside also influences whether you utilize HealthCare.gov or a state marketplace to enroll in 2024 health insurance.

When you sign up influences when your health insurance plan begins.

In most situations, you have to enroll by December 15 if you want your health insurance plan to begin at the start of the new year. So if you acquired coverage during last year's open enrollment, signing up for a plan by December 15 guarantees you'll avoid a lapse in coverage.

2024 health insurance changes

In 2024, there are two key developments happening that relate to health insurance enrollment dates.

Special enrollment for losing Medicaid and CHIP: If you have lost coverage via Medicaid or the Children's Health Insurance Program (CHIP), you may have unique health insurance enrollment alternatives. Marketplace sites might enable you to get coverage up to 60 days before losing Medicaid or CHIP coverage, or up to 90 days after.

Avoiding gaps in coverage: Sometimes, you could know you're about to lose your health insurance coverage at a future date. Marketplaces now offer the option to start your plan sooner so you may avoid a lapse in coverage.

There are also certain adjustments that have to do with re-enrolling in the same health plan.

Bronze-to-Silver crossing policies: If you presently have a Bronze-level plan but you would be eligible for cost-sharing reductions on a Silver plan, you could be re-enrolled in the Silver plan instead.

The Silver plan has to be the same price or less than your Bronze plan and has to use the same network of doctors. Essentially, you may automatically receive better coverage for the same or a lesser price.

Network similarity: If your existing health plan is no longer accessible, your insurance provider has to identify a comparable doctor network to re-enroll you in a plan.

You may pick a new plan manually, but if you allow the system to re-enroll you, your firm needs to place you in a plan with a comparable doctor network as your former policy.

In 2024, you could also be able to obtain enrollment support at home. Trained health insurance specialists, called Navigators and Assisters, could previously only teach you about health insurance policies. Now, they can really assist you in enrolling.

Chapter 6: Rules for Health Insurance

In prior years, you had to obtain qualified health insurance coverage or pay a charge. This was dubbed the health insurance requirement. But the regulations have changed in recent years, and you might not be forced to buy insurance anymore.

Federal rules: While health insurance is still theoretically needed, there's no federal penalty for being uninsured. In most jurisdictions, you won't be fined if you don't buy insurance, but certain states have different restrictions.

State rules: A state-level mandate exists in California, Massachusetts, New Jersey, Rhode Island, Vermont, and Washington, D.C., making health insurance a necessity for those people.

Even if there is no government obligation, it's crucial to obtain health insurance to prevent the high expense of health care. Without health insurance, you might wind up emptying out a savings account or needing to borrow money to cover medical expenditures.

Some Americans also put off preventative care if they don't have health insurance, which can lead to more serious health difficulties later on. Having health insurance coverage is a critical component of taking care of your physical and financial health.

Chapter 7: What is Health Insurance Copay

A health insurance copayment, commonly referred to as a copay, is a predefined fixed amount that an insured individual is obliged to pay out of pocket for specified healthcare services or prescription prescriptions covered by their health insurance plan.

Copayments are one of the ways in which the expense of healthcare is split between the insured person and the insurance company.

Typically, copayments are paid for many sorts of medical services, such as doctor's office visits, specialist consultations, emergency department visits, and prescription drugs. For example, if you had a $30 copay for a primary care physician (PCP) visit, you would be responsible for paying $30 each time you see your PCP, regardless of the overall cost of the appointment.

Copayments serve numerous roles within health insurance:

1. Cost-sharing: Copayments help divide the financial burden of healthcare between the insurer and the insured. They aim to reduce the overutilization of medical services by requiring patients to take some financial responsibility for their treatment.

2. Predictability: Copays give a degree of predictability for insured persons since they know in advance how much they will owe for certain healthcare treatments.

3. Managing healthcare expenses: Insurers employ copayments to limit costs by encouraging consumers to choose lower-cost treatment alternatives when appropriate. For example, choosing a generic prescription with a cheaper copay

instead of a brand-name drug with a higher copay.

4. Encouraging preventative treatment: Some health insurance plans provide free or reduced copays for preventive services like immunizations and screenings to encourage customers to prioritize preventive care.

It's vital to understand that copayments are unique from other cost-sharing schemes, such as deductibles and coinsurance. Deductibles are the amount you must pay out of pocket before your insurance starts paying charges, while coinsurance is a percentage of the total cost of a treatment that you are liable for.

The particular copayment amounts and the services they apply to can vary widely between insurance plans, so it's vital to study your policy documentation to understand your copay obligations. Additionally, some plans may offer exclusions or waivers for specific preventative treatments or vital prescriptions to ensure that patients may get necessary care without financial restrictions.

Chapter 8: What is OPM Health Insurance

OPM health insurance, or the Federal Employees Health Benefits Program (FEHBP), is a comprehensive health insurance program provided to federal government workers, retirees, and their qualified families. Administered by the U.S.

Office of Personnel Management (OPM), this program is a crucial aspect of the federal employee benefits package. Here's a more extensive look at OPM health insurance:

1. Wide Range of Options: One of the program's defining aspects is its varied choices of health plans. These plans exist in many varieties, including Health Maintenance Organizations (HMOs), Preferred Provider Organizations (PPOs), and Fee-for-Service (FFS) plans. This

diversity allows individuals to pick a plan that best matches their healthcare requirements and preferences. Each year, during the Open Season, participants can examine their alternatives and modify strategies if required.

2. Coverage for Government Employees and Retirees: OPM health insurance primarily targets federal government employees, including current and retirees. Federal retirees can maintain their coverage through this program, providing they fulfill particular qualifying conditions. This continuity of coverage is highly appreciated since it ensures that retirees may continue access to comprehensive healthcare services.

3. Employer Contributions: A big advantage of OPM health insurance is the financial support offered by the federal government. The government provides a percentage of the premium expenses for these programs,

lessening the financial load on members. The actual amount of the government's contribution is regulated by legislation, and it is a fundamental benefit of the program.

4. complete Coverage: OPM health insurance policies normally provide complete healthcare coverage. This covers hospitalization, doctor's visits, prescription medicines, preventative care, and more.

The comprehensive extent of coverage guarantees that members have access to a wide range of medical treatments, encouraging overall health and well-being.

5. Portability: OPM health insurance frequently permits individuals to continue their coverage when they leave federal work, as long as they satisfy particular standards. This portability is especially useful for retirees who may not have access to employer-sponsored health coverage after leaving their federal professions.

6. reasonable Pricing: Due to the huge and diversified pool of federal employees and retirees participating in the program, OPM health insurance plans can generally negotiate reasonable prices and offer cost-effective alternatives compared to individual market policies. The program's scale and bargaining strength assist participants by keeping rates more cheap.

In short, OPM health insurance is a strong and adaptable healthcare program designed to satisfy the requirements of federal government employees, retirees, and their families.

Its emphasis on choice, affordability, and comprehensive coverage has made it a valued benefit for people who have served or are now serving in the federal workforce. Participants can access a variety of health plans, enjoy considerable employer contributions, and have the option to alter plans to fit changing circumstances. This initiative emphasizes the government's commitment to the health and well-being of its employees and retirees.

Chapter 9: PPO Health Insurance

A PPO, or Preferred Provider Organization, is a form of health insurance plan that offers a balance between flexibility and cost savings for healthcare services. PPOs are a popular choice among many individuals and families owing to their adaptability and general availability in the United States. Here's a full look at what PPO entails in health insurance:

Provider Network: PPOs have a network of preferred healthcare providers, which includes physicians, specialists, hospitals, and other medical facilities.

These providers have agreed to offer their services at negotiated rates to PPO plan subscribers. While you are not compelled to pick a healthcare provider inside the network, utilizing one often leads to cheaper out-of-pocket payments.

versatility: One of the primary advantages of PPOs is their versatility. Unlike HMOs (Health Maintenance Organizations), which normally require users to pick a primary care physician and acquire recommendations to see specialists, PPOs enable you to see any healthcare provider, both in-network and out-of-network, without having referrals. This flexibility is appealing to consumers who seek greater control over their healthcare decisions.

Out-of-Network Coverage: PPOs give some coverage for out-of-network services, however, the cost-sharing structure is less attractive than for in-network treatments. When you obtain treatment from out-of-network providers, you often pay a higher deductible, coinsurance, and copayments. Despite this, the ability to consult experts or access services that may not be offered in-network might be valuable to certain individuals.

No Primary Care Physician Requirement: PPOs do not need you to pick a primary care physician (PCP) or acquire referrals to see specialists. You can independently book appointments with experts or seek medical treatment without a PCP's participation. This streamlines the procedure and provides for speedier access to healthcare services.

Cost-Sharing: In a PPO plan, cost-sharing methods such as deductibles, copayments, and coinsurance are typical. Deductibles are the amount you must pay out of pocket before the insurance starts paying expenditures.

Copayments are set amounts you pay for particular services (e.g., $20 for a doctor's visit), whereas coinsurance is a percentage of the overall cost of treatment (e.g., 20%

for a hospital stay). The particular cost-sharing parameters vary on your plan.

Premiums: PPO plans generally have higher monthly premiums compared to HMOs or other forms of plans. This is because they give greater freedom in picking healthcare providers and provide out-of-network coverage. Participants pay a charge to keep access to these perks.

Coverage for Preventive Care: Like other forms of health insurance plans, PPOs often include preventive care at no cost to the participant. This includes immunizations, tests, and preventive health checkups.

In short, a PPO (Preferred Provider Organization) health insurance plan allows flexibility in choosing healthcare providers, allowing you to see specialists and access out-of-network treatments without referrals. While it may have higher monthly premiums compared to certain other plans, the trade-off is greater control over your healthcare decisions. PPOs are a popular alternative for people who desire the freedom to pick their physicians and specialists and are ready to pay slightly extra for that flexibility. However, it's vital to research the exact details of your PPO plan, including provider networks, cost-sharing, and out-of-network coverage, to make educated healthcare decisions.

Conclusion: Your Path to Financial and Physical Wellness

As we come to the end of this fascinating voyage through the complex world of health insurance, it's important to reflect on the knowledge learned, misconceptions debunked, and tools offered to navigate the ever-changing environment of healthcare coverage. In "Navigating Health Insurance," we set out to turn health insurance from a puzzling conundrum into a powerful tool for health and financial stability.

We've learned throughout this book that health insurance is more than just a financial transaction; it's a lifeline that connects us to a world of healthcare options. It is the safety net that catches us when we fall, the protector of our bodily and financial well-being, and the gateway to a better, more confident future.

We've decoded the jargon of health insurance, from deductibles to copayments, premiums to out-of-pocket maximums. We've equipped you with the information to make educated decisions about the sort of coverage that best meets your needs, whether you're a solitary adventurer or a family experiencing life's twists and turns together.

But, above and beyond the nitty-gritty, we've gotten to the core of the matter: the significant influence that health insurance can have on your life. It is the piece of mind that comes from knowing you may seek medical treatment without worry of financial ruin. It is the flexibility to select healthcare providers based on your needs and choices, rather than merely what your insurance requires. It's the comfort that your family's future is secure, even if unexpected health difficulties arise.

As you conclude the final chapter of this book, keep in mind that health insurance is a dynamic instrument that may adapt to your changing circumstances. Use everything you've learned here to constantly analyze and adjust your coverage, ensuring it stays in line with your aims and aspirations.

Your quest for financial and physical well-being is continuous. You are well-equipped to handle the hurdles, grasp the possibilities, and harness the power of health insurance to create a life of security, independence, and well-being with the wisdom taught in these pages. Here's wishing you continued good health, happiness, and success. Best wishes on your journey to a better tomorrow!